New York (State) Commission

The Tennessee Centennial

A Souvenir of the Trip Taken by the Brooklyn Party and the New York...

New York (State) Commission

The Tennessee Centennial
A Souvenir of the Trip Taken by the Brooklyn Party and the New York...

ISBN/EAN: 9783337145064

Printed in Europe, USA, Canada, Australia, Japan

Cover: Foto ©Andreas Hilbeck / pixelio.de

More available books at **www.hansebooks.com**

THE
TENNESSEE
CENTENNIAL

Published by the
New York State
and Brooklyn Commissioners
Eighteen Hundred and
Ninety-eight

A SOUVENIR of the Trip taken by the Brooklyn Party and the New York State Commissioners to attend the "Brooklyn Day," and the "New York State Day" Exercises at the Nashville Exposition, October Eighth to October Fifteenth, Eighteen Hundred and Ninety-seven.

5

PREFACE.

Merely a few notes about a Southern pilgrimage, printed by direction of members of the party who desired some lasting memento calculated to refresh their memory in years to come.

THE TENNESSEE CENTENNIAL

᪲᪲᪲᪲᪲᪲

THE Nashville excursion of 1897, under the auspices of the Brooklyn Commission and the New York State Commission, was a source of pleasure to every participant. It is not the purpose of this sketch to present a complete record of events from the inception of the movement which resulted in the Southern jaunt to the last step of the homeward journey, but rather

BIRD'S-EYE VIEW OF EXPOSITION.

to give a running account of the main features of the trip, and to recount a few of the many pleasant incidents.

In the first place, October 11, 1897, was Brooklyn Day at the Nashville Exposition, and October 12 was New York State Day. The State Commissioners named by Governor Morton were: John C. Eames, New York, President; Timothy L. Woodruff, Vice-President; Geo. F. Kunz, New York,

SARACEN'S TENT, LURAY CAVERNS.

Treasurer; John C. Latham, New York; Robert R. Hefford, Buffalo; Herbert F. Gunnison, Brooklyn; James Swann, New York; Dr. Frank R. Vandenberg, Buffalo; Titus Sheard, Little Falls; Stephen P. Corliss, Albany; and A. M. Wheeler, Secretary.

The Brooklyn Commissioners named by Mayor Frederick W. Wurster were as follows: William Hester, William M. Van Anden, Charles A. Schieren, William Perri, George A. Price, Charles A. Moore, William M. Wallace, F. S. Sherry, Daniel T. Wilson, A. D. Baird, Robert P. Lethbridge, J. Henry Dick, Ernestus Gulick, Thos. P. Peters, Richard Young, William C. Redfield,

GOVERNMENT BUILDING.

THE OFFICERS OF THE BROOKLYN COMMISSION.

LIEUTENANT-COLONEL LUSCOMB AND STAFF.

William Vogel, Herbert L. Bridgman, Ludwig Nissen, A. E. Palmer, Charles E. Wheeler, G. P. Bagnall, Robert J. Wilkin, James McLeer, John D. Keiley, Augustus Van Wyck, Dr. A. N. Bell, Abraham Abraham, H. B. Scharmann, James McKeen, C. C. Broun, William C. Pate, George P. Jacobs, A. H. Angell, F. M. Munroe, James A. Sperry, W. H. Baldwin, Jr.; A. W. Higgins, D. P. Watkins, Herman Schaeffer, Charles H. Russell, Dr. Albert H. Brundage, Mrs. Cornelia H. Cary, Miss Ellen A. Ford, Mrs. Augustus Van Wyck, Mrs. A. G. Brown, Mrs. C. N. Chadwick, Miss Alice Campbell, Mrs. Mary E. Craigie, Mrs. Benjamin F. Stephens, Mrs. James Scrimgeour, Mrs. E. L. Langford, and Mrs. Clara McCrory Dorsey. Mrs. Charles N. Chadwick resigned from the Commission, and Mrs. E. L. Langford declined to accept her appointment.

The women members of the Brooklyn Commission were appointed a committee on exhibits, and that committee organized as follows: Mrs. Cornelia H. Cary, Chairman, and Miss Ellen A. Ford, Secretary; Mrs. Augustus Van Wyck, Mrs. A. G. Brown, Miss Alice Campbell, Mrs. Mary E. Craigie, Mrs. Benjamin F. Stephens, Mrs. James Scrimgeour, and Mrs. Clara McCrory Dorsey.

Before going into the work of the main commission, and the account of the excursion itself, it should be stated that the women commissioners did valiant service from first to last. The Committee on Exhibits collected some excellent photographic views of characteristic Brooklyn scenes, and sent them on to be hung in the Women's Building, but the Southern officials refused to hang them, on the ground that they were "not appropriate for a woman's work exhibit."

THE BROOKLYN EXHIBIT.

COL. WILLIAM HESTER,
Member of the Brooklyn Commission

The pictures found a place, however, in an alcove of the Commerce Building, and so, though the exhibition as planned was a disappointment, the efforts of the committee were not in vain, by any means.

The State Commissioners arranged a program for New York Day, but decided to make the trip South with the Brooklyn party, and to leave all the details to the officers and Executive Committee of the Brooklyn Commission. Those officers and that committee were as follows: Herbert F. Gunnison, President; William C. Redfield, Secretary; Ludwig Nissen, Treasurer. Executive Committee: William Berri, Chairman; Daniel T. Wilson, A. Abraham, George A. Price, Andrew D. Baird, John D. Keiley, and Thomas P. Peters.

In passing over the preliminary part of the record, it is only fair to say that, although the Brooklyn Commission arranged all the details, and carried out all the working plans, the New York State Commission paid its full share of the expenses, and lent cordial and effective aid to the enterprise in many ways. Without the co-operation of the

ORGAN ROOM, LURAY CAVERNS.

MRS. AUGUSTUS VAN WYCK   MISS ELLEN A. FORD

MRS. A. G. BROWN   MRS. CLARA McCRORY DORSEY

MRS. MARY E. CRAIGIE   MRS. BENJ. E. STEPHENS

MRS. C. H. CARY

COMMITTEE ON EXHIBITS OF THE BROOKLYN COMMISSION.

gentlemen comprising the State Commission, the excursion could hardly have been the brilliant success it was.

The Executive Committee held many meetings; the Secretary indulged in reams of delicately phrased correspondence; conferences were held with railroad officials, musicians, soldiers and others concerned; and, altogether, a great deal of very hard work was done before the plans were perfected.

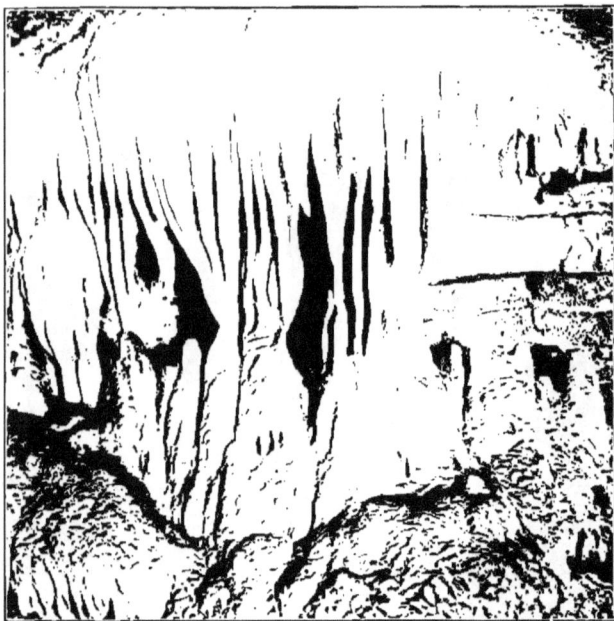

STALACTITE AND STALAGMITE FORMATIONS IN LURAY CAVERNS.

One important feature proposed and successfully carried out was the addition to the Brooklyn party of a provisional battalion, under command of Lieutenant-Colonel Luscomb, made up as follows: Twenty-five men from the Thirteenth Regiment, commanded by Captain Harry A. Williams; twenty-five men from the Fourteenth Regiment, commanded by Captain John F. Carroll; also, twenty men

WOMEN'S BUILDING.

from the Twenty-third Regiment, commanded by Captain Charles G. Todd; ten men from the Forty-seventh Regiment, detailed; nine men from Troop C, commanded by Sergeant Charles Curie, and four men from the Signal Corps, commanded by Sergeant Verdi E. B. Fuller. The

COMMERCE BUILDING.

battalion staff was as follows: Adjutant, Lieutenant G. P.
Bagnall; Quartermaster, Captain E. J. Olden; Commis-
sary, Captain T. H. Avery; Assistant Commissary, Captain
H. C. Barthman; Inspector of Rifle Practice, Captain E. J.

Kraft; Surgeon,
Captain A. R. Jar-
rett. This battal-
ion went to Nash-
ville and returned
by special train,
and served as an
escort to the
Brooklyn and
New York State
Commissioners
during the two
days' exercises.

The committee
in charge of the
general plans de-
cided on this
route: From New
York *via* Pennsyl-
vania Railroad to
Harrisburg; *via*
Cumberland Val-
ley Railroad to
Hagerstown;
Norfolk and West-
ern Railroad to
Luray, Va., Nat-

THE NATURAL BRIDGE.

ural Bridge, Roanoke and Bristol; *via* Southern Railway
to Knoxville and Chattanooga; *via* Nashville, Chattanooga
and St. Louis Railway to Nashville, returning *via* Louisville
and Nashville Railway to Glasgow Junction, Mammoth

DANIEL T. WILSON.

A. ABRAHAM.

JOHN D. KIELEY.

THOMAS P. PETERS.

GEORGE A. PRICE.

ANDREW D. BAIRD.

EXECUTIVE COMMITTEE OF THE BROOKLYN COMMISSION.

KNOXVILLE BUILDING.

Cave, Louisville and Cincinnati; *via* Pennsylvania Railway to Pittsburgh, Harrisburg and New York.

Events afterward proved that the final stage of the route was: *via* Brooklyn Heights Railroad system, special parlor cars, to the Eastern District, South Brooklyn and Flatbush.

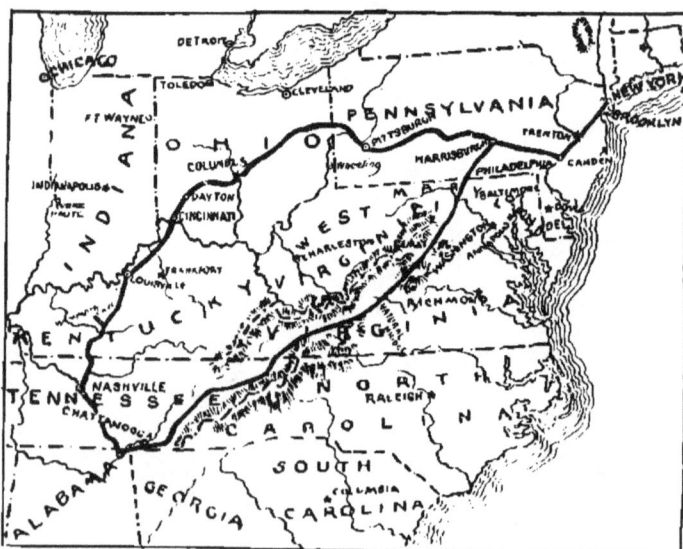

MAP OF THE ROUTE.

EN ROUTE TO NASHVILLE.

The start was made on Friday evening, October 8th, from the Pennsylvania Depot in Jersey City. One of the finest special trains ever made up carried the party around the "long loop" to Nashville and return. The Committee had provided for each member of the party a book of tickets covering every step of the journey, and it was a model of beauty and convenience.

There was no hitch in getting away, the only disappointing feature being the inability of Chairman Berri to join the party and the sudden illness of Mrs. Timothy L. Woodruff, just prior to the start, which made it necessary for the Lieutenant-Governor and his wife to remain a day longer in Brooklyn. They arrived in Nashville in time for the Brooklyn Day exercises, and returned with the main party.

As the special rolled out of Jersey City it carried the following passengers:

THE BROOKLYN BADGE.

Henry S. Adams, A. D Baird, Mrs. A. D. Baird, George W. Baker, M. D.; Hon. Charles G. Bennett, George P. Bergen, Mrs. George P. Bergen, Mrs. L. P. Bodkin, A. G. Brown, Mrs. A. G. Brown, William C, Bryant, Mrs. William C. Bryant, Pomeroy Burton, J. Ambrose Butler, Benj. T. Butterworth, Isaac H. Cary, Mrs. Isaac H. Cary, Stephen P. Corliss, C. O'H. Craigie, Mrs. C. O'H. Craigie, John L. Cummings, Mrs. W. H. Cummings, P. J. DeCantillon, William C. DeWitt, Mrs. William C. DeWitt, Walter Dunham, G. B. Ellis, Mrs. G. B. Ellis, L. J. Ellis, Bernard Gallagher, Miss Amelia Gallagher, Miss Augusta Gallagher, Ernestus Gulick,

3

GEORGE W. BAKER, M. D.,
Physician to the Party.

Herbert F. Gunnison, Mrs. Herbert F. Gunnison, Joseph W. Hawkes, Mrs. Joseph W. Hawkes, Robert R. Hefford, Mrs. Robert R. Hefford, William Hester, Hugh M. Inman, Seth L. Keeney, John D. Keiley, Mrs. John D. Keiley, T. W. Kiley, George F. Kunz, Mrs. George F. Kunz, R. P. Lethbridge, John Loughran, Miss Loughran, Charles H. Lyons, Mary E. McCann, St. Clair McKelway, Mrs. St. Clair McKelway, Henry N. Meeker, Mrs. Henry N. Meeker, C. G. Moller, Mrs. C. G. Moller, Thomas F. Morrin, Ludwig Nissen, Mrs. Ludwig Nissen, W. A. Porter, Mrs. W. A. Porter, Neil Poulson, Mrs. Neil Poulson, Mrs. Bernard Peters, T. P. Peters, Mrs. T. P. Peters, George A. Price, Mrs. George A. Price, John Pullman, Miss Nettie I. Pullman, H. F. Quast, Mrs. H. F. Quast, A. V. V. Raymond, D.D., William C. Redfield, Mrs. William C. Redfield, Miss Elsie M. Redfield, A. B. See, Don C. Seitz, Titus Sheard, Mrs. Titus Sheard, D. A. Smith, Mrs. D. A. Smith, Benjamin F. Stephens, Mrs. Benjamin F. Stephens, Mrs. F. E. Story, James Swann, J. G. Tuthill,

TRANSPORTATION BUILDING.

JOHN C. EAMES, PRESIDENT.

TIMOTHY L. WOODRUFF, VICE-PREST.

ALGAR M. WHEELER, SECRETARY.

GEORGE F. KUNZ, TREASURER.

THE NEW YORK STATE COMMISSIONERS.

A SHADY RETREAT.

William Vogel, Mrs. William Vogel, Miss Etta Vogel, A. A. Voorhees, Judah B. Voorhees, Albert Wesley, J. E. Williams, Timothy L. Woodruff, Mrs. Timothy L. Woodruff, Frederick W. Wurster, Mrs. Frederick W. Wurster.

The Itinerary, which was closely followed, was thus outlined in the little ticket book:

GOING.

October 8. —Leave Jersey City, 10 P. M.

October 9.— Arrive Harrisburg, 3 A. M.; leave Harrisburg, 3.05 A. M.; arrive Hagerstown, 5.20 A. M.; leave Hagerstown, 5.25 A. M.; arrive Luray, 8.25 A. M. (stop three hours at Luray); leave Luray, 11.25 A. M.; arrive Natural Bridge, 2.55 P. M. (stop three hours at Natural Bridge); leave Natural Bridge, 6 P. M.; arrive Bristol, Eastern time, 12 midnight; arrive Bristol, Central time, 11 P. M.; leave Bristol, Central time, 11.05 P. M.

October 10.—Arrive Chattanooga, 5.35 A. M. (stop at Chattanooga); leave Chattanooga, 12 noon; arrive Nashville, 5 P. M.

RETURNING.

October 13. — Leave Nashville, 12 midnight.

October 14 —Arrive Glasgow Junction, 2.45 A. M.; leave Glasgow Junction, 7 A. M.; arrive Mammoth Cave, 7.45 A. M. (stop four hours at Mammoth Cave); leave Mammoth Cave, 11.45 A. M.; arrive Glasgow

Junction, 12.30 A. M.; leave Glasgow Junction, 12.40 A. M.; arrive Louisville, 3.10 P. M. (stop at Louisville); leave Louisville, 5 P. M.; arrive Cincinnati, 8.25 P. M.; leave Cincinnati, 8.45 P. M.

October 15.—Arrive Pittsburgh, Central time, 5.35 A. M.; arrive Pittsburgh, Eastern time, 6.35 A. M.; leave Pittsburgh, Eastern time, 6.45 A. M.; pass Horseshoe Curve, 9.35 A. M.; arrive New York, 6.53 P. M.

All the Brooklyn papers sent representatives with the excursion, who sent daily reports to their respective journals regarding the progress of the party and events *en route*. The *Standard Union* and Brooklyn *Life* were represented by Mr. Henry S. Adams; the *Citizen*, by Mr. P. J. De Cantillon; the Brooklyn *Times*, by its editor, Mr. T. P. Peters, and its publisher, Mr. William Cullen Bryant; the *Eagle*, by Col. William Hester, President; Mr. St. Clair McKelway, Editor-in-Chief; Mr. Pomeroy Burton, Associate Managing Editor; Mr. Herbert F. Gunnison, Assistant Business Manager; Mr. Benjamin T. Butterworth, Manager of the *Eagle* Information Bureau, and Mr. Harry B. Wilson, Special Representative.

The first night on the special was a smooth and comfortable experience. The travelers awoke to find themselves whirling through picturesque Northern Virginia, and shortly

THE RIALTO.

HON. CHARLES G. BENNETT,
Member of the Brooklyn Commission.

after breakfast had been served the first stop was made at Luray. The stop of three hours there was all too short; but, though much had to be left unseen, the hour which the party spent in the wonderful cavern was one of rare enjoyment. Near the close of the journey, when the home-stretch was being entered by the giant Pennsylvania flyers which pulled the Brooklyn special, the tourists were asked to name the feature or features which had pleased them most. Perhaps, a score of the number named Luray Cavern as the most notable of all their experiences.

On reaching the train the members of the party were surprised to learn that a miniature traveling edition of the Brooklyn Daily *Eagle* had been printed at Luray while they were exploring the cave. To be sure, the first page was printed upside down, and there were typographical combinations terrible to behold; but, nevertheless, within the three hours the edition was put in type and printed, and as it contained

ERNESTUS GULICK,
Member of the Brooklyn Commission.

JOHN C. LATHAM.

ROBERT R. HEFFORD.

STEPHEN P. CORLISS.

TITUS SHEARD.

JAMES SWANN.

DR. FRANK P. VANDENBERG.

HERBERT F. GUNNISON.

THE NEW YORK STATE COMMISSIONERS.

news about the previous night's journey and a few
words from home, it was welcomed by all and its defects
were overlooked. The paper proved one of the interesting features of the trip, and on the two big days at
Nashville it contained the only complete reports published
of New York and Brooklyn day exercises. With experience,
the traveling edition improved from day to day, as plans for
overcoming the mechanical obstacles incident to printing on

BIRD'S-EYE VIEW OF EXPOSITION.

the wing were gradually perfected, and before the end of the
week the news by wire from home, the record of the party's
doings, the personal quips, and the illustrations, serious and
otherwise, were eagerly looked for as publication hour arrived. The regular publication hour, by the way, was something which the publishers themselves failed to discover.
All that they can vouch for is the fact that not a mail was
missed during the week. The little paper's editorial page
announcement was as follows:

BERNARD GALLAGHER,
Attorney at the Mock Trial.

Brooklyn Daily Eagle.
(TRAVELING EDITION.)

This paper does not claim much of a circula-tion, but it has more rolling stock than any other paper in the United States.

Main office, Brooklyn, N. Y. Branch offices, Luray, Va.; Chattanooga, Tenn.; Nashville, Tenn.; Louisville, Ky.; Harrisburg, Pa.

Communications accompanied by stamps will be destroyed and the stamps will be used by the editor.

At the head of the news page was the customary form of business announcement, thus:

Brooklyn Daily Eagle.
(TRAVELING EDITION.)

THE TRAVELING EDITION of this paper is published as often as convenient. For the time being it is a try-daily.

TERMS OF SUBSCRIPTION.

We will send you the paper for a week free of cost, and if at the end of that time you are still in your usual good health, we will suspend publication.

BACK NUMBERS.

We have a few distinguished back numbers in our party, but they are not for sale.

COMMUNICATIONS.

Address all communications to the Editor of the TRAVELING EDITION OF THE EAGLE, and hand MSS. to the porter, with instructions to collect on delivery—if he can, which he can't, for how can he? The Editor will be glad to receive complimentary letters from all the members of the party.

WILLIAM VOGEL,
Member of the Brooklyn
Commission.

Dinner was served in the two handsome dining cars in the course of the run from Luray to Natural Bridge. There the primitive and somewhat Wild Western stage facilities proved inadequate, and some of the party had to wait a

4

MACHINERY BUILDING, FROM LAKE WATAUGA.

long time at the station before they could be transported over the rugged route to the Bridge. The delay was taken in rare good humor by the unfortunate section which was left behind, but the Committee was grievously disappointed to encounter so serious a mishap that early in the

ARBOR LEADING TO AUDITORIUM

program. However, it was the only grievance that the Committee or those in the Committee's charge encountered in the course of the whole trip, and in the rush of good things the single sorrow was soon forgotten.

The Natural Bridge was worth the struggle it cost, and the afternoon's experiences gave all a hearty appetite for dinner.

At Chattanooga next day the excursionists formed two parties, which chose different routes for sight-seeing. One

TERMINAL STATION.

went up the most wonderful inclined cable road in the land to famous Lookout Mountain, and the other, under the skillful and entertaining guidance of Colonel A. D. Baird, took carriages and drove over historic Missionary Ridge. It was Colonel Baird's old fighting ground, and his modest recital of stirring events in which he had participated was made doubly interesting by the fact that his listeners gazed, as he talked, on the very ground where those events had transpired upward of two score years before.

THE PARTHENON.

Up on Lookout Mountain the other division was having a fine time. The thrilling journey up the mountain side and the series of grand views from the summit were all enjoyed to the utmost. Mayor Wurster was of this party, and when Chairman Gunnison pointed out the spot where a monument was to be raised in honor of Colonel Lewis R. Stegman, the Brooklyn soldier who first scaled the great rock when the Confederates were driven from

ROBERT P. LETHBRIDGE,
Member of the Brooklyn Commission.

Lookout Mountain, his Honor proposed that an impromptu monument be built with no further delay, and carried the first stone to serve as its base. Each member of the party

A BIT OF SHADE.

contributed his share, and soon the monument was erected.
A cheer went up as the capstone was placed on the pile by
Colonel James Swann, of New York, who had been an officer
in the Confederate army. The Mayor made a speech form-
ally dedicating the pile, and an appropriate inscription was
printed and fastened upon it. The incident was one of the
most interesting of the whole trip. The monument still
stands as an evidence of the excursionists' appreciation of
Colonel Stegman's valor.

MINERALS AND FORESTRY BUILDING.

The run from Chattanooga to Nashville was made under
conditions most pleasant. Those who had engaged rooms
at the hotel left the train when it reached the Union Depot,
but the majority of the travelers remained in their comfortable quarters on board the special, and as they slept were
transported right to the Exposition grounds, and side-
tracked within fifty yards of the main entrance. So ended
the first part of the journey by rail.

The party was welcomed on the night of arrival by Mr.
Justi, of the Bureau of Publicity, and other officials of the

Exposition, and it should be stated that during the entire stay the Fair officials did all in their power to entertain the Brooklyn party.

Brooklyn Day began dark and rainy; but by ten o'clock the clouds had broken, and a half hour later, when the line was formed at the Maxwell House, the sun was shining and all was bright. The procession was headed by the Troop C detachment and the other military bodies comprising the provisional battalion. Then followed twenty-five carriages

AUDITORIUM.

containing Mayor Wurster, the Commissioners and other members of the Brooklyn party, together with a few invited guests.

The Brooklyn Day exercises were held in the great Auditorium. They were opened with an appropriate address by Herbert F. Gunnison, President of the Brooklyn Commission.

Mayor William M. McCarthy, of Nashville, responded in a happy address of welcome, and Mayor Frederick W. Wurster, of Brooklyn, replied, speaking at length on "The City of Brooklyn."

In part Mayor Wurster said:

"It affords me the utmost pleasure to appear as the representative of the City of Brooklyn to respond to the cordial greeting extended on behalf of the City of Nashville by his Honor the Mayor. I am also delighted to stand here as the spokesman for this representative body of Brooklynites, who have traveled a long distance hither to participate in the celebration of the day set apart in honor of their city, as well as to see the manifold beauties of this superb exposition.

"While the name of Brooklyn may not be as well and widely known as those of some of the other cities of our land, yet it will soon possess the unique distinction of sinking its individuality entirely by union with New York and becoming part of the greatest city on this continent. After the close of this year the City of Brooklyn will be the Borough of Brooklyn, one of the five sub-divisions of the City of New York. While the plan of consolidation which will make New York the second city of the world in size includes a large amount of outlying territory, yet it is practically the union of the present cities of Brooklyn and New York.

"In all well regulated marriages the bride becomes the 'better half,' and we are fully justified in saying that Brooklyn will be the 'better half' of New York.

"I am glad to see Brooklyn so well represented here upon the occasion of the day set apart for our city. The pressing exigencies of public affairs and private business are responsible for the fact that there is not a larger representation. We are filled with admiration for the energy and ability shown in the management of so great an enterprise as this exposition, commemorating the beginning of your great State. To the people

HISTORY BUILDING.

CHILDREN'S BUILDING.

who have had the opportunity to see what you have brought together for their benefit this should prove of great educational value. To us of the North who have come a thousand miles to see what the South can do, this is a revelation of the extent of territory and the capacity of the people of our common country. We rejoice that you have found the way to do so much to show the world that to no one section of our land are confined the qualities that insure success in every enterprise undertaken.

"On behalf of the City of Brooklyn I heartily congratulate the people of Nashville, and especially the management of this Tennessee Centennial Exposition, upon the success attained, and express the confident hope that the ultimate results may prove to be all that could be wished. Permit me to thank you, Mayor McCarthy, and the officers of this exposition, for the courtesies extended to the representatives of Brooklyn, both by the City of Nashville and the Centennial Commission. We shall take to our distant homes many pleasant memories of this trip to the sunny South, and especially of our stay in this charming City of Nashville."

The salutation of Mr. J. W. Thomas, President of the Exposition, next engaged the attention of the listeners. It was an earnest address of welcome and made a most favorable impression.

William C. Redfield, Secretary of the Brooklyn Commission, followed in reply to President Thomas. He spoke with good effect and was warmly applauded.

5

MRS. MARGARET E. SANGSTER,
Poet on Brooklyn Day.

The poet of the occasion was Mrs. Margaret E. Sangster, who was greeted with much enthusiasm as she stepped forward on the platform to read "Pilgrims." This commanded the closest attention and was adjudged by all to be one of the notable features of the day's proceedings. The poem was published in many of the leading newspapers and periodicals of the country, and was especially praised by the Nashville press. The full text of the poem is herewith reproduced.

PILGRIMS.

By Margaret E. Sangster.

" Pilgrims with staff and scrip, pilgrims with eager faces,
Pilgrims who take the road and search out hidden places,
Pilgrims with eyes intent on gold, until they find it;
Pilgrims on pleasure bent, no other aim behind it;
Grave pilgrims, wistful, wise, and pilgrims young and merry;
Girl pilgrims, blushing sweet, with cheeks and lips of cherry,
Still as in elder days, of song and of thrilling story;
Pilgrims crusading go, for joy, or fame, or glory.

" From where the white surf breaks on the shore of old Long Island,
By winding burns and rills, by valley, stream and highland,—
Pilgrims with staff and scrip, we have sought a city, queenly,
Fair on her river banks, dwelling in state serenely,—
A city of people brave, whom all the land must honor,
As meekly she lifts her head, with praises thick upon her.

" Once in the dim rich streets of Camelot, famed forever,
Wonderful pageants passed, fading from memory never.
Once and again we've seen tower and palace lifted,
And thither have art and life in gallant argosies drifted ;
The pomp and splendor wane, but the story of pluck and power,
Told for the thousandth time, lives on to the deathless hour.

" Rich is the city still, with its myriad clustering spires,
Its thronging friendly doors, and its genial household fires ;
To the city all things come, its gates are wide and fair,
And the roads, wherever you find them, are always leading there.

" People of Tennessee, brothers, we come to greet you ;
Glad is the word we speak, our hearts speed forth to meet you
Under October's sky, with the regal banners flying,
Red and gold on the trees, and the roses sweet ere dying ;
We are proud one land is ours (oh ! beautiful, great land,
Godward and childward looking !), under one flag we stand,
And the blood-bond holds us close,—we are one and kindred hearted ,
Never by alien hands shall the dear love-tie be parted ,
Blood is thicker than water, · 'tis this we say to thee
As we gather in thy doorway, beautiful Tennessee."

THE NEGRO BUILDING.

ST. CLAIR McKELWAY, LL.D.,
Orator on Brooklyn Day.

The orator of the day was St. Clair Mc-Kelway, LL.D., editor of the Brooklyn Daily *Eagle*. He was warmly greeted, and spoke in his best vein. His address, which appeared in full in all the local papers of that date, was eloquent and forceful, and was received with great favor by all who heard it. The opening paragraphs were as follows:

" A city speaks to a city when Brooklyn speaks to Nashville. A self-governing community speaks to a self-governing community when Brooklyn speaks to Tennessee. Yet not for long can this be so. Our salutatory to you is our valedictory to ourselves. We are here on parole, but under sentence of municipal death. The fact invests this occasion with a pathos which those who are the Brooklyn part of that occasion find it hard to forget. Nevertheless, we bring to you the best wishes of twelve times one hundred thousand Americans, and, without boastfulness, we can claim that we are citizens of no mean city. Ours is a city of which the religious spirit is as benign as the fatherhood of God and as broad as the brotherhood of man. Ours is a city of homes whose purity has become a proverb, and whose fecundity has become a cynicism to the enemies of posterity. Ours is a city of schools as well as of churches, of homes, of colleges and of institutes. These together are building up in minds and in souls and in lives temples fit for the indwelling of the Holy Ghost. We could name to you clergymen whose eloquence has given to them continents for congregations ; physicians whose skill has increased the duration of human life ; soldiers whose valor has been impaired by no vengeance and stained by no venality ; scientists who have advanced the race in its knowledge of the works of God ; financiers who have solved more serious problems in economics than now divide American thought ; discoverers who have carried the American heart and the American flag nearer to the limit of the planet than either was ever taken before ; merchants who have opened the gates of the antipodes to the energy of the world ; reformers who have dared to do right with the approbation of a community which regards party as an instrument and not as an idol—as a factor and not as a fetich ; diplomats who have insisted with success and with dignity upon the right of Americans to the rights of human nature across the seas and around the globe—and many others who, as a great cloud of witnesses, look down on us to-day in the hope that the children of the new dispensation shall be worthy heirs of the moral riches of an imperishable past.

DR. ALBERT H. BRUNDAGE,
Member of the Brooklyn Commission.

"I cannot, with justice or with propriety to time or place, recount or even runningly summarize this illustrious roll of our Brooklyn names. Nor shall I descend to pessimism or to reproach in contemplating the transition of Brooklyn from cityhood to boroughhood. Those with whom I am and for whom I speak would have had the result otherwise. Small, however, as was the vote by which the question went against us, as good Americans we bowed to the decision of the majority and are turning our faces toward the morrow in a spirit of hope. We would that the apprehensions and predictions of evil with which we fought this change may never be realized. We would not be vindicated in that way. Our further hope is that the promised benefits of municipal merger, which have not yet come and which do not yet appear upon the horizon, may, nevertheless, soon come and fully come, filling all with help and heart as the impartial sunlight of the serene heavens. We would have our opponents vindicated rather than ourselves, and will outdo them in works for the common weal, if so be we can bring, as men and women do often bring, the best answer to our own best prayers. We know that we can give to New York not only more than she now has but, better, a something which she most lacks and most needs. We can give to her the element of an independent citizenship as to which the average material circumstances are those neither of poverty nor of riches, and the moral influence of which, upon the over rich and upon the over poor of the commercial metropolis, should make for good.

"We cannot think of ourselves in the same way that we think of you. Brooklyn is to become a leaven hidden in four borough measures of metropolitan meal, until the whole be leavened. The heart of a great community among us might compare its progress, but it cannot discuss its problems, with yours. Our past may parallel yours on the path of achievement, but our future record will go to the increment of an artificial system lately created by experimental legislation into which suffrage is yet to breathe the breath of life. On the contrary, your Nashville, your Memphis, your Chattanooga, your great State of Tennessee, on whose brow those diamond cities are worn in beauty and in strength, will go on from much to more, not unheralded and not unsung. Take, then, our congratulations that you have saved your life. You cannot realize how sweet and precious your life is, for you are not parting with it. But cherish it as the immediate jewel of your soul. Covet none of the gains or seeming gains that are made the alternative to a reduction of liberty or to the loss of autonomy. Individuality in the man, in the city, in the State is the need and will be the salvation of the time. Not the selfishness which substitutes combination for manhood, and which merges the man in the mass, but the selfhood which raises worth above wealth, personal purpose above bundled power, and the culture of the heart above the aggrandizement of the pocket should be the note sounded in the ears of Americans to-day. The example which you set—the warning which we present and are—should not be lost."

Dr. McKelway was frequently applauded in the course of his address. When the outburst which followed his closing remarks had subsided, Mrs. Bernard Peters was presented. She spoke as the representative of the Brooklyn women, and her words made a most favorable impression. She said, in part:

"Expositions, such as this in Nashville, show the place woman holds in the realm of industry. It is a question yet unsettled whether woman ought to have her corner alone or whether she ought to exhibit her work side by side with man's work, and let it be judged on its own merits, rather than to be accorded a notice with this implied, if not expressed, idea—pretty good for a woman. But what, after all, is the worth of honorable mention, certificates and medals, if they do not represent something of use? Use should be the touch-stone of all we do or acquire. To be of use to home and country should be the aim of each and every woman, especially of the women of these United States, for nowhere in the world is woman accorded the place and the honor that is conceded to her in our own dear native land. Here woman has the opportunity to be useful. She can make our country a land of liberty, not license; a land of independence, not impudence. She can be a builder of the home, and thus a benefactor of the world.

"She will be loved, honored, venerated. She will be the uncrowned queen. Then will be seen a world where everyone will be content. Great enterprises for the good of all will be undertaken, 'where one mind suffices for a thousand hands.' Then every invention for physical comfort, every appliance for intellectual and æsthetic culture, all means for spiritual improvement, will be free, and peace and plenty will be the portion of every human being, from the highest to the lowest in the land."

The address of Mrs. Peters closed the Brooklyn Day exercises.

In the evening there was a brilliant reception in the New York State Building. The New York State Commission supplied the music and refreshments, but all the arrangements were made by the women of the party, and to them belong full credit for the complete success of the affair. The State Building was tastefully decorated and brilliantly lighted.

MRS. BERNARD PETERS,
Speaker on Brooklyn Day.

The company included a number of fair guests from Nashville society. Several pleasant informal addresses were made in the course of the evening. About 9 o'clock Mrs. Cornelia H. Cary, Chairman of the Ladies' Committee, stepped into a space which had been cleared directly under the New York State emblem and addressed the company.

MRS. FREDERICK W. WURSTER.

Mrs. Craigie followed with an address that was beautiful in its simplicity, both as to structure and delivery, and masterly in its strength. Unfortunately, a verbatim report of her words was not taken, but a partial report was published in the traveling edition of Tuesday, Oct. 12th.

NEW YORK STATE DAY.

The next morning—and a bright, cheery morning it was—the New Yorkers and Brooklynites joined forces to celebrate New York Day at the Exposition. The military escort headed the long line of carriages, as on the day previous, and the procession moved, as it had done before, from the Maxwell House to the Exposition grounds, and then the party repaired to the Auditorium.

Governor Taylor, of Tennessee, opened the New York Day exercises with an exceedingly felicitous address of welcome. Among other things he said:

"New York is the Empire State of the Union. She is the heavy end of North America, she is the great throbbing heart of the Republic, and every time she throbs the life current of the nation flows back and forth through the arteries of commerce and trade. She is the mighty whale of the Western hemisphere which swallows all the Jonahs who come within her reach. She is the stupendous colossus of the world, leading its thought and straddling its politics

"The city of New York is a perpetual exposition of the triumphs of thought and industry, and one of her grandest products is men. She is the paradise of millionaires and enjoys a considerable sprinkling of poor folks.

THE KENTUCKY BUILDING.

HEALTH AND HYGIENE BUILDING.

"New York is not only great in wealth, great in population, great in all the elements of modern civilization, but she is great in the knowledge of where the green pastures lie.

"It is believed by many of our brethren of the North that our people here in the South are not as vigorous as we should be, that we lack the snap and push necessary for the quick and permanent growth and development of our country. But they forget that we can raise three crops of potatoes in our soil in a single season, that our cotton grows without much persuasion, that we can fatten our hogs on acorns, and pasture our cattle the year around. They forget that our persimmon trees yield tons of persimmons per annum, and that the 'possums hang like sugar lumps of glory hallelujah from the bending limbs of the aforesaid and the same. They forget that we can labor half the time and rest the other half and live better and happier than any other people on the face of the earth.

"There is one branch of business in which we are as vigorous as our Northern brethren, and that is politics. Our annual crop of politicians is equal to the crop of cotton bales, not in weight, but in numbers. Now and then we are blessed with a statesman, but many are called, but few are chosen. We produce more Majors and Colonels, in times of peace, than any other country in the world, and, sometimes, we raise a little of that sulphurous article which begins with an h and ends with an ell.

"But, whatever the differences between the North and the South may be in climate, in wealth, in conditions and environments, we are all one people with common hopes, and a common destiny, and may God bless our people of every section. Again I implore you to feel that you are welcome to the capital of the Old Volunteer State."

6

TIMOTHY L. WOODRUFF,
Lieut.-Governor State of New York.

Lieutenant-Governor Timothy L. Woodruff, of New York, responded, dealing with Northern and Southern topics of interest.

Here are a few extracts from the Lieutenant-Governor's speech:

"To us of New York the names of your famous statesmen and generals are household words. They illustrate the history of your State from its genesis to its present greatness. Some of our electors still persist in voting for your greatest son, whose name of 'Hickory' and victory is known world-wide. Nor have James K. Polk, Andrew Johnson, John Bell, Horace Maynard or the eccentric Parson Brownlow been forgotten. We are aware that there are in the nation's archives muster rolls innumerable of the sons of Tennessee, which attest the splendor of their volunteered valor in over a hundred battlefields. The great conflict, in December, 1864, before this very city of Nashville, is not to be surpassed in the Civil War for the skill and bravery displayed. I am gratified, every loyal American must be, to think of Tennessee's roll of honor as embraced in the Confederate Army of the Tennessee, under its various commanders from Bragg to Hood, and in its splendid achievements from Bowling Green, Shiloh and Murfreesboro to Chickamauga and Chattanooga.

"We must not forget the renowned cavalry leader, General Forest, of whom General Sherman said, when he offered his services to the Union in the threatened Spanish emergency in 1874 'I shall recommend him to the very highest position to which he can be appointed, if the occasion is necessitated, to prove my high admiration of his almost unequaled genius in his particular sphere in war.' It is also pleasant for every American to remember the text of the beautiful letter of the son of the sainted Lincoln, who, as Secretary of War, offered to the State of Tennessee an official transcript of all who had served in its regiments.

"And now that I, a loyal citizen and representative of a Northern State, have given expression to the sentiments that dominate the minds of my fellow citizens concerning the State of Tennessee and its illustrious representatives on the field of national politics and on the field of war, a sentiment bids me pause, which was expressed by an old Indian chief of the Cherokees

on the occasion of the signing of a treaty with the early settlers of Tennessee :
'A little talk is as good as much talk, and too much talk is not good. We
hope to live friends together and to keep our young men at peace, as we are
agreed to sign and live in peace forever hereafter.'

"Ladies and gentlemen, in conclusion, permit me to say that the State of
New York extends heartiest greetings to the State of Tennessee. May your
State pride spurn all sectional lines and insist upon hearty unity, born of the
fiery furnace of a great conflict for our mutual national progress.

"Nashville sits more proudly than ever on her many hills, with no frown-
ing fortifications or menacing soldiers to mar her career. The busy hum of
industry follows the supremacy of law and order, and a happier era flows
naturally where might does not subvert the right. Love will long linger

A STATE BUILDING.

over fields consecrated by the slain. But the Union, cemented again by the
best blood that ever flowed, is not restored in vain, when, to all the genera-
tions of the side that lost, as well as of the side that saved, comes that new
and higher birth of freedom which Lincoln proclaimed."

Dr. James H. Kirkland, Chancellor of Vanderbilt Uni-
versity, then spoke briefly, and was followed by the chosen
orator of the day, Dr. Andrew V. V. Raymond, President of
Union College, New York, who began as follows:

"The State of New York brings to the State of Tennessee a greeting and
a message ; congratulation, admiration, affection join in the greeting ; good

DR. A. V. V. RAYMOND,
Orator on New York State Day

will and godspeed in the message. In the presence of these splendid tokens of your progress, the hand which your sister State extends to you is warm and tense with honest pride and heartfelt praise. Only a great, intelligent, enterprising people, commanding vast and varied resources, could create this impressive scene. In all that tells of knowledge and skill, of energy and enthusiasm, of virtue and refinement, we see the prosperous and enlightened commonwealth which commands the tribute of admiration so freely given, but we cannot forget that these achievements of the present are, also, memorials of the past bearing virtue to the courage and sacrifice of the fathers, who laid deep and strong the foundations upon which the children have built through a hundred years. The secret of American greatness is found not alone nor chiefly in the boundless material resources of this western world, but is written large in the masterful spirit of the men who came hither to subdue and transform. The magic of their touch has made the wilderness to blossom as the rose. The vigorous qualities of their splendid manhood have come down through the years, conquering and still to conquer. Looking back upon the colonists of New York and the pioneers of Tennessee we miss many of the externals of greatness, the familiar accompaniments of place and power, but stripped of these accessories of life in older and settled communities the essential qualities of dominant natures stand out only the more boldly."

The oration, which was scholarly and eloquently delivered, was published in full in the daily papers of Brooklyn and Nashville.

The closing address was made by William C. DeWitt, of Brooklyn. Mr. DeWitt devoted his whole attention to the patriots of the South, and therein lay the secret of his success. He touched a sympathetic chord in the Southern mind, and his speech elicited much applause, and called forth many favorable comments afterward. He said, in part:

"You may rest assured, my countrymen of Tennessee, that there are very many in the far Northern land from which I came, who, during the struggles, privations and hardships of the recent past, have felt for you the utmost fraternal solicitude and affection.

"They are a band of intelligent patriots who early imbibed that philosophy, of which Jefferson and Calhoun are the chief exponents, and who even now, when the last vestige of civil war is passing away, doubt whether the two races are any better off than they were in the olden times, and more than apprehend that the one hundred million people who are soon to inhabit our wide domain cannot be governed by the centralized system of Hamilton, rather than by a feder-

HON. WILLIAM C. DE WITT,
Speaker on New York State Day.

ation of sovereign States, agreeable to the principles for which your kindred fought and died.

"But everybody lies under the deepest debt of gratitude to Tennessee for her three great Presidents—Jackson, Polk and Johnson!

"Andrew Jackson was the irresistible friend and champion of the common people. Swept on to power by their responsive patriotism, no form of plutocracy could stand before him. He overthrew the National Bank, and smashed every monopoly that came within his reach. He was vilified and abused through life by every instrumentality that sordid greed could influence and inspire, but his body sleeps to-day not more securely at the Hermitage than is his memory embalmed in the heart of every lover of mankind. Nor can the less brilliant but no less efficient service of James K. Polk be displaced from the highest rôle of American patriots.

"It was to the impetus of his campaign for the Presidency, dictated by Jackson, that we owe the acknowledgment of the independence of Texas, the Lone Star State, under the guidance of their mutual friend, old Sam Houston. Three such heroic souls would long ago have given independence to Cuba. Under President Polk the war against Mexico was declared. Under him, as commander-in-chief, occurred that series of victories which carried our flag to the halls of the Montezumas; and under him was dictated those terms of peace which added California, Utah, Arizona and New Mexico—a vast and golden empire—to our possessions. Now, too, when the clouds have rolled away, everybody can see what a debt of gratitude the nation owes to Andrew Johnson.

"Citizens of Tennessee! Great men and the popular support of great

STATUE OF MINERVA.

men make a State. The glories of your Centennial Exposition will soon pass away. But the characters of these three great men are enduring, like your majestic mountains the works and benefactions of their lives flow on forever, like your bountiful rivers in their unending pilgrimage to the sea."

At the conclusion of the New York Day exercises, dinner was served, and then the party broke up into sightseeing groups, some preferring to "do" the fair grounds, others to explore the country roundabout, and a large delegation choosing to avail itself of a golden opportunity to enjoy a taste of real Southern hospitality through invitations which had been extended by President and Mrs. J. W. Thomas and by Colonel and Mrs. Edmond W. Cole. The "Traveling Edition" of the next day thus described the trip:

"The Brooklyn and New York party were given on Tuesday an opportunity to enjoy some of that generous hospitality for which the warm-hearted Southern people are so famed. They were all invited to attend two receptions during the afternoon, one given at 'Colemere' the charming country seat of Colonel and Mrs. Edmond W. Cole, and the other at the delightful home of President J. W. Thomas, head of the Exposition. As 'Colemere' is some six miles out of Nashville, the guests were taken there in tally-hos and open carriages, leaving the Exposition grounds at 2.30. The way led through a beautiful wooded, hilly section, and the winding country road, with its hundred or more carriages, varied by the bright

gowns of the ladies in their best attire, presented a picture that quite
fulfilled the ideal of Southern social life.

"'Colemere,' a typical Southern country home, is a stately gray stone
mansion, approached by a private drive, leading through a magnificent
park of rare old trees. As Mayor Wurster and his party entered the gate, a
band stationed on the lawn played popular airs that enlivened the scene.

"The receiving party consisted of Mrs. Edmond W. Cole and her mother,
Mrs. Russell, Mrs. Washington Roebling, Mrs. John A. Logan, Mrs. L. B.
Bodkin, Mrs. Ella Wheeler Wilcox, Mrs. Lyndhurst and other women
prominent in Nashville. Among the guests were many prominent men and
women of the literary world, who were present from the Congress of Artists
and Authors, and who had been in session at the Exposition during that day.

"From 'Colemere' the party drove to Capitol Hill, to the residence of
President and Mrs. Thomas.

"Receiving with Mrs. Thomas were Miss Bailey, the authoress, of New
York; Miss Gilmer, of New Orleans, and a charming bevy of the young
ladies of Nashville.

"The generous hospitality which was extended through these receptions
in two of the most prominent homes in Nashville afforded the party an
excellent opportunity to obtain a glimpse of the social life for which Nashville is so famed, and resulted in the formation of many pleasant friendships
between the ladies of the North and South."

Wednesday forenoon was spent in general sightseeing,
both within and outside of the Exposition grounds.
Many members of the party enjoyed the warm hospitality
of the Hermitage Club, and also of the Riding and Driving

INTERIOR OF THE AUDITORIUM.

"UNCLE BOB" AFTER ROUNDING UP THE DEER AT BELLE MEADE FARM.

Club, both of which took pains to make everything pleasant for the visitors from the North.

Immediately after luncheon the Brooklyn party left the city on a special train for a visit to the famous Belle Meade Stock Farm, located six miles from the city, where they were escorted over the grounds by the owner and manager, General W. H. Jackson. In their honor the General ordered a deer drive, showing the visitors nearly two hundred wild deer dashing over the fields and through the woodland at full speed. Then the famous horses were exhibited. Among the animals shown were Iroquois—considered to be the most valuable horse in the world, who is valued at $250,000— Longstreet, Tremont, and Luke Blackburn. Next the party inspected the dairy, one of the most notable of the Belle Meade sights, and on the way back to the special, a favored few stopped at the homestead long enough to sip genuine Southern mint juleps, made after the General's own formula.

This charming little excursion to Belle Meade was due to the thoughtfulness and courtesy of Mr. J. H. Fall, who added much to the pleasure of the party during the stay in Nashville. The special train on this particular afternoon was arranged for by him, and its use was extended in the name of himself and his fellow Directors of the Nashville, Chattanooga and St. Louis Railway Company.

Those of the travelers who did not go to Belle Meade farm attended a charming reception given by Mrs. Van Leer Kirkman at her beautiful Oak Hill mansion on the Franklin Pike. It was a delightful experience to all who participated.

That evening the last rounds were made in the Exposition grounds; once more all the quarters on the luxurious special were occupied, and at midnight the start was made for home.

The "American" and the "Banner," the two leading newspapers, printed daily accounts of the doings of the party while in Nashville.

SNAP SHOT TAKEN AT THE DEPOT AT BELLE MEADE FARM.

ENTRANCE TO MAMMOTH CAVE.

THE HOMEWARD RUN.

The night run to Glasgow Junction was made without special incident. After breakfast the little branch train which runs from the Junction to Mammoth Cave was crowded with the excursionists, and in a short time all were preparing for the trip to the lower regions.

The men donned costumes terrible to behold, and some of the ladies took to bloomers. Altogether it was a grotesque procession which entered the hole in the ground a half hour after the party arrived at the hotel. One of the guides unfeelingly remarked that the Brooklyn party looked like a line of well-fed convicts and bouncing bloomer girls. Only a few miles of the Cave were traversed, owing to the limited time, but the journey underground was extremely interesting so far as it went.

From Glasgow Junction a fast run was made to Louisville, where a three hour stop enabled the travelers to see considerable of the city. On the way to Louisville Mr. Redfield, at the request of several of the ladies, made up a progessive

MARTHA WASHINGTON STATUE, MAMMOTH CAVE.

euchre party, and a shopping committee, when the stop was
made, purchased the following prizes: First prize for men,
corkscrew with ivory handle, mounted with sterling silver;
women's prize, ivory glove stretcher, mounted with sterling
silver.   Second prize for men, silk hat brush with solid silver
handle; women's, tortoise-shell comb, mounted with sterling
silver.   Consolation prize for men, silver bell with carved

THE GIANT'S FINGER IN MAMMOTH CAVE.

ivory handle; consolation prize for women, crescent-shaped
match-striker, with darkey's head, engraved "Looking for
light." The committee which brought the prizes also pro-
cured the cards, a conductor's punch, sixty tally cards with
red and white ribbons, and returned to the train triumph-
ant, with ninety cents in the treasury.

At 8 o'clock in the evening a merry company assembled in the dining car Coronado, which had been tastefully decorated for the occasion. The play was spirited, and there was great fun throughout the evening, the prizes finally being awarded as follows: First prize for women, won by "Miss" Burton; second, by Mrs. H. F. Quast. First for men, won by Mr. W. A. Porter; second, by Mr. George P. Bergen. The consolation prizes were won by Mrs. Vogel and Dr. Baker.

THE GRANITE FACE, MAMMOTH CAVE.

After Cincinnati was left behind a good night's rest was enjoyed, and every member of the party awoke refreshed and eager for the promised pleasure of the last day's run over the picturesque mountain region of Pennsylvania. Two of the most powerful engines of the Pennsylvania line pulled the special out of Pittsburgh, and an average of fifty miles an hour was maintained to Altoona, and thence on to

STONE HUT BUILT BY CONSUMPTIVES IN MAMMOTH CAVE.

Harrisburg, and through, via Trenton, to New York. At Harrisburg the closing number of the *Eagle's* traveling edition was issued.

The feature of the afternoon on the train was a mock trial in the observation car. Ludwig Nissen was charged with having withheld and appropriated for his own use the sum of $17.50, which was said to have belonged to Mayor Wurster and H. F. Gunnison, said sum having been withdrawn from circulation in a wrongful and malicious manner by said Nissen's accomplices, Timothy L. Woodruff and Bernard Gallagher, the last named being also accused in the same complaint of stealing a rattle from the Mammoth Cave snake on Friday, October 15, 1897. St. Clair McKelway was the sitting judge before whom the case was tried. He denied the motion for a change of venue on the ground of the versatility of criminality which characterized the chief conspirator for the defence. There were many sharp sallies in the course of the proceedings, and Mr. Nissen made an impassioned plea in his own behalf, which only succeeded in bringing upon him the wrath of the court, and a sentence of interminable parole in the custody of his wife. Mr. Gallagher acted as attorney for the plaintiffs.

It is interesting now to look back upon a straw vote which was taken in the observation car that afternoon, with a view to ascertaining which one of the Greater New York mayoralty candidates was the favorite of the party. Sixty-seven votes were cast in all, of which twenty-two were non-voters. The ballot stood as follows:

For Low, 46 votes—28 voters ; 18 non-voters.
For Tracy, 14 votes—11 voters ; 3 non-voters.
For Van Wyck, 3 votes—2 voters ; 1 non-voter.
Votes, scattering, 4.

Jersey City was reached on time, and there the first good-bys were said. The Brooklynites crossed the Bay on the Annex boat, and were pleasantly surprised to find two special parlor cars awaiting their coming. This climax of good things was the result of a happy thought on the part of Seth L. Keeney, who, together with William C. Bryant, Major John D. Kieley, directors of the Brooklyn Heights Railroad Company, had telegraphed ahead to have cars at the ferry when the excursionists arrived. One car went to the Eastern District of the city, the other to Flatbush, and so the Nashville travelers continued to ride by "special" to their doors.

THE PARTHENON.

MAYOR WURSTER'S COMMENT.

When Mayor Wurster reached his desk in the City Hall next day after he returned home he was asked by the reporters what he thought of the Southern jaunt. He said:

"The trip was a complete success. Everything passed off without a hitch. It is wonderful that on a journey of 2,000 miles everything should have gone so smoothly. The most pleasant feature was the company on the train. They were all Brooklynites of the most companionable kind, and the associations were delightful. The visit to Luray Cavern was a revelation, and I would advise every one who may be in a position to do so to visit the place. It affords the most magnificent spectacle I have ever witnessed. As to the

Nashville Exposition, I can only say that it was most wonderful when you take into consideration that it was simply a State demonstration. The building was splendid, the exhibits were complete and the arrangements generally were of the most perfect character. The Exposition certainly reflects great credit upon the managers. I cannot speak too highly of the courtesies shown by the citizens of Nashville to the Brooklyn party. We were the recipients of many invitations to the houses of prominent people, whose hospitality was unbounded. Incidentally I wish to speak of the visit we paid to the Belle Meade stock farm, owned by General Jackson, who received

MAMMOTH CAVE, STAR CHAMBER.

us most cordially, and, after showing us about the place, afforded us an opportunity to witness a genuine deer chase. I wish, also, to speak of the work done by the Brooklyn commissioners appointed by me, and, especially, the ladies. They seemed to appreciate the importance and responsibility of their position and worked diligently to make our trip a success. I likewise take advantage of this opportunity to thank the provisional guardsmen of Brooklyn for their escort and for their efforts to make the excursion successful, and to give evidence of the civic pride of Brooklyn. We heard on all sides from citizens of Nashville, that the delegation from Brooklyn was the best, the most intelligent and the most representative body of citizens who have as yet visited the Fair."

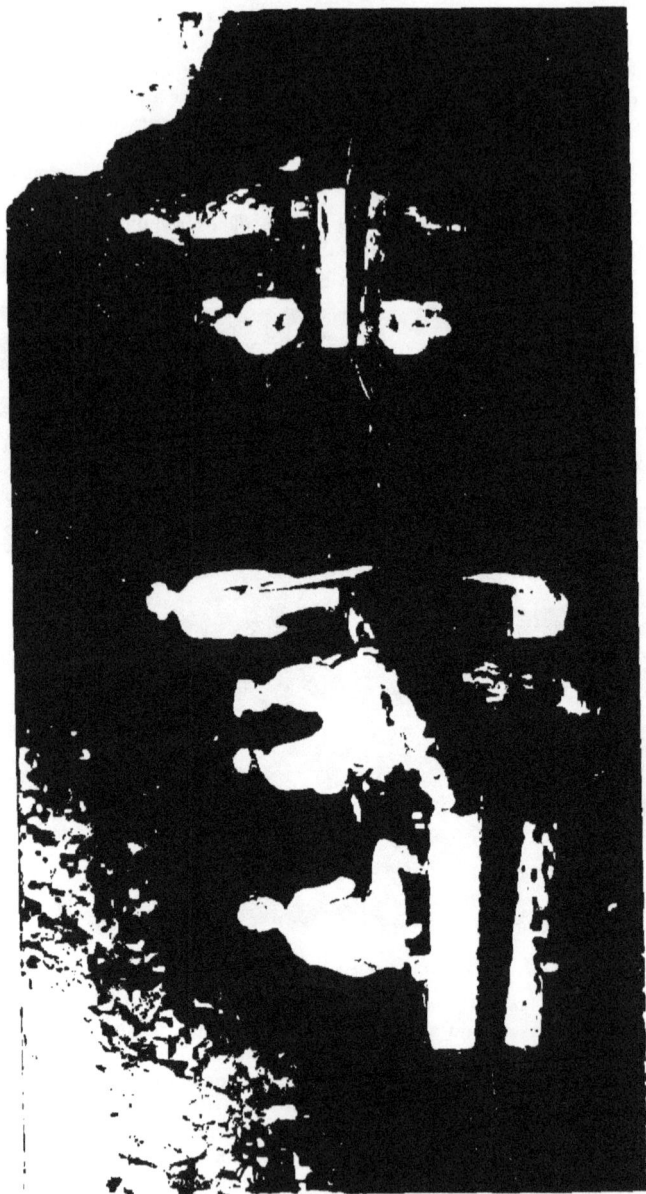

BOATING ON ECHO RIVER IN MAMMOTH CAVE.

THE SOLDIERS' JOURNEY.

Regarding the trip of the Brooklyn soldiers, the *Eagle* had this to say the day after their arrival home:

"The Brooklyn Provisional Battalion of the National Guard, which went to the Nashville Exposition, returned last night, after their week's trip of 2,000 miles. The men were all in good condition, and seemed sorry that their outing was over. While crossing the river homeward, on the South Ferry, the guardsmen gave vent to their enthusiasm in long cheers for Lieutenant-Colonel Luscomb, the commander of the battalion, and, in

NEW YORK STATE BUILDING.

response to their call for a speech, he stated that the trip was a record breaker, and that it would go down as such in the history of the National Guard. Colonel Luscomb complimented the men and thanked them on behalf of the officers in command for their unswerving attention to duty, their prompt attendance at assembly and gentlemanly behavior and soldierly deportment through all the scenes of the long journey.

"The battalion, on its special train, passed through nine States and the District of Columbia, stayed over night in Baltimore and Cincinnati on the way to Nashville, affording the men a chance for sightseeing, and were two days at the Exposition in Nashville, parading in fatigue uniform on Brooklyn

Day, through the rain, and in their dress uniform on New York Day, their splendid appearance on all occasions causing much favorable comment. In Nashville and Washington the guardsmen were thought to be regulars— quite a compliment to their marching and drill.

" From Nashville the battalion went to Mammoth Cave, Ky., stayed at the hotel over night and next morning, in a body, explored the subterranean caverns, and embarked in boats on the dark waters that flow in the lowest level of the great cave. From Mammoth Cave the run was made to Washington, D. C., the party reaching there Thursday night. The battalion was received in the east room of the White House on Friday morning by President McKinley, and at 1 30 the march was made to the special that conveyed the guard home. The train accommodations on the whole trip were good and the men sent a testimonial of thanks and appreciation to the Baltimore

ILLINOIS STATE BUILDING.

and Ohio and Lackawanna and Western railroads and to the passenger agents of both lines, who accompanied the battalion. There were about one hundred in the party, twenty-five men from the Thirteenth Regiment, commanded by Captain Harry A. Williams; twenty-five men from the Fourteenth Regiment, commanded by Captain John F. Carroll; also, ten men from the Forty-seventh Regiment, under the same command; twenty men from the Twenty-third Regiment, commanded by Captain Charles G. Todd; nine men from Troop C, commanded by Sergeant Curie, and four men from the Signal Corps, commanded by Sergeant V. E. B. Fuller. The battalion staff was as follows: Adjutant, Lieutenant G. P. Bagnall; quartermaster, Captain E. J. Olden; commissary, Captain T. H. Avery; assistant commissary, Captain H. C. Barthman; inspector of rifle practice, Captain E. J. Kraft; surgeon, Captain A. R. Jarrett."

SPLENDID RAILROAD FACILITIES.

In conclusion, a few words should be said about the excellent railroad facilities which the Brooklynites enjoyed during their week's absence from home. No small part of the success of the trip was due to the service rendered by the lines over which the party traveled. To say that it was good would be putting it mildly. The arrangements made by the Pennsylvania, Norfolk and Western, the Southern, the Nashville,

A ROOM IN THE WOMEN'S BUILDING.

Chattanooga and St. Louis, and the Louisville and Nashville Railroads to take care of the Brooklyn party were simply perfect, and each road seemed to vie with the others in doing everything possible to add to the comfort of the travelers. Leaving the Pennsylvania depot at Jersey City five minutes late Friday, October 8th, the run to Philadelphia was made on schedule time, with only one engine to pull the heavy train of nine massive Pullman cars. At this

9

STAIRWAY IN WOMEN'S BUILDING.

point an extra engine was added to pull up the heavy grades
to Harrisburg, and it required two engines all the way to
Nashville.

The first day's ride was through the beautiful Shenan-
doah Valley, in the scenery of which the Norfolk and Western
Railroad may well take pride. Mr. L. J. Ellis, the Eastern
Passenger Agent of the road, accompanied the party and
did the honors while traveling on his line. Two of the big-
gest wonders in North America, the Luray Caverns and the
Natural Bridge, on this road, were duly inspected and highly
appreciated by the party. From Bristol, Tenn., to Chattanooga the run was made over the Southern Railway, a representative of the road joining the party at Bristol, and the
party was treated to some pretty fast traveling. The scenery
on this part of the route is most beautiful, but the run was
made during the night while all but a few "night hawks" on
the rear platform of the observation car, were sound asleep.

The Nashville, Chattanooga and St. Louis Railway took
the train in charge at Chattanooga, and took most excellent

care of it, not only on the run to Nashville but during the
three days the party stopped at the centennial city. The
ride to Nashville over this line was through one of the finest
sections of Tennessee, over mountains and through fertile
farming districts. The time made was better than scheduled,
and the party arrived in Nashville early in the evening.
This road did more to accommodate the Brooklyn party
than it did for any other special train during the Exposition
season. It parked the cars right at the Fair grounds, convenient to the entrance gate and the downtown city trains,
switched the train several times a day so as to enable the
crew to stock up with ice and water, and showed many other
unusual courtesies. Special permits were issued to a number
of the party stopping at the hotel in the city to bring their
trunks to the Exposition grounds on the suburban trains.

Leaving Nashville at midnight Wednesday last, the trip
to Mammoth Cave and Cincinnati was made over the
Louisville and Nashville Railroad, and Mr. John E. Burke,

LIBRARY IN WOMEN'S BUILDING.

the Eastern Passenger Agent of the road, who accompanied
the party back to New York, is authority for the statement
that it is the " only railroad " in the *South*. However, no
one argued the point with him. The Louisville and Nashville is certainly a fine road on which to travel, the rails are
of the heaviest, steadiest and smoothest, and the entire system is thoroughly rock ballasted. Mr. Burke had reason
to be proud of the record breaking run which was made

A BEDROOM EXHIBIT.

between the cave and Cincinnati, a large portion of the journey being made at the rate of over fifty miles an hour.

At Cincinnati the special was delayed two hours to
get a new supply of gas for the cars. To make up this
time the Pennsylvania Railroad attached its most powerful engines and made a wonderful run to Pittsburgh,
where only a short stop was made. From Pittsburgh to
New York the train fairly flew over the ground and around
curves, over mountains and through valleys. The time was
so fast, the motion made by flying around curves caused a

few people to feel as though they were on shipboard. Mr. D. A. Smith, Traveling Passenger Agent of the Pennsylvania Railroad, accompanied by his wife, made the round trip. Next day it was Mr. Smith's turn to talk, while Mr. Burke said nothing. Mr. Smith went Burke one better and thought there was only one railroad in the *country* and that was the Pennsylvania. Two engines hauled the train over the mountains and around the Horseshoe Curve to Altoona, after which point only one was needed on the down grade. In order to save time and about twenty five miles in distance, the Pennsylvania Road arranged to run the train over the Trenton cut-off, thereby leaving out Philadelphia. The Jersey City depot was reached shortly after 8 o'clock, very near to the time originally scheduled. Great assistance was also rendered the Commission by Samuel Carpenter, Eastern Passenger Agent of the Pennsylvania Railroad in New York, and Mr. W. W. Lord, Jr., his assistant, and also by Mr. Alexander Thweatt, Eastern Passenger Agent of the Southern Railroad in New York.

Another word of praise is due the service and equipment furnished the Brooklyn party by the Pullman Palace Car Company. There was probably never a finer train of cars made up by this company. The combination baggage and smoker was complete in every detail, and contained a barber shop and a bath-room. The state-room and drawing-room cars were models of convenience, and contained all the comforts of a modern hotel room. The dining car service was of the very best, and the menus were excellent. The train was in charge of Conductor C. F. Hammet, who was remembered by many of the party most pleasantly as the genial conductor of the Atlanta special two years before. The dining car stewards, porters, waiters, cooks and messengers were from the oldest and most able corps of the Pullman working force. They were polite, courteous and thoroughly alive to the wants and comforts of the excursionists. Mr. Duncan, the efficient head of the Commissary Department of the Pullman Company, accompanied the party.

ROSTER OF THE PROVISIONAL BATTALION.

The following are names of the members of the Provisional Battalion that acted as escort to the Brooklyn and New York Commissioners:

Thirteenth Regiment—Lieutenant-Colonel Chas. H. Luscomb, field; Captain A. R. Jarrett, staff; Captain H. A. Williams, Company G; First Lieutenant J. T. Ashley, Company G; Second Lieutenant T. D. Croffutt, Company B; Sergeant-Major T. M. Harvey, Quartermaster-Sergeant A. Klar and Ordnance Sergeant J. McNevin, N. C. S.; First Sergeant F. W. Nash, Company G; First Sergeant Geo. Smith, Company E; Quartermaster-Sergeant A. I. Eason, Company G; Sergeant E. Lovenberg, Company G; Sergeant J. H. Morris, Company F; Corporal A. T. Johnston, Company A; Private H. J. Moeller, Company C; Private J. C. Arnott, Company D; Private A. Winant, Company D; Privates L. B. Becker, J. Manneschmidt, M. P. Cook, A. L. Conklin, Jr., and Clarence Ryder, Company G; Private J. P. Stagg, Company K; Musician E. S. Mansfield, Company B.

LIEUTENANT-COLONEL LUSCOMB,
Commanding the Provisional Battalion.

Fourteenth Regiment—Captain John F. Carroll, Company F; Captain T. H. Avery, Company C; First Sergeant Geo. P. Eldridge, Company C; Commanding Sergeant, Ramon Cardona, Ordnance Sergeant P. Farrell and Sergeant-Major W. J. Mullin, Non-Commissioned Staff; Sergeant Thomas

Rome, Company I; Sergeant J. W. Creighton, Company F; Sergeant David Thorne, Company C; Sergeant Wm. Headrich, Company F; Corporal F. A. Evealand, Company D; Corporal Geo. Reynolds, Company F; Privates A. E. Burrill, John Dubois, Frank Pearce, John D. Foote, T. A. Hooper, Company C; John R. Edwards and H. H. Wilkinson, Company A; A. N. Edlund, Company G; Musician Peter A. Nealis, Company C; Musician E. H. Beardsley, Company I; Musician W. E. Hines, Company H.

Twenty-third Regiment — Captain C. G. Todd and Lieutenant W. J. Travis, Company K; Ordnance Sergeant Chas. E. Bryant, N. C. S.; Sergeant E. Codet, Company K; Sergeant J. P. D. Shiebler, Company H; Corporal A. R. Boerum, Company K; Corporal F. G. Sinzheimer, Company H; Privates F. DeR. Boerum, W. R. French and W. F. Hillman, Company K; Private W. N. Kenyon, Company D; Private A. H. Shiebler, Company A; Private J. F. Tormey, Company C; Private F. H. Whitlock, Company K.

LIEUTENANT G. P. BAGNALL,
Member of the Brooklyn Commission

Forty-seventh Regiment—Captain H. C. Barthman, Company I; Captain E. J. Olden, Company B; Sergeant-Major W. J. Wilson and Color Sergeant J. E. D. Breen, N. C. S.; Corporal R. R. Miller, Company F; Corporal C. F. Way, Company I.

Signal Corps—Sergeant Verdi E. B. Fuller, Privates John R. Smith, Reginald W. Earle and Palmer H. Jadwin.

Supernumerary—First Lieutenant G. P. Bagnall.

Troop C.—Sergeants Charles Curie, Jr., and Edw. H. Walker, Veterinary Sergeant W. H. Pendry, Trumpeter Louis Barrett, Privates Lewis G. Langstaff, F. A. Lane,

A VIEW OF EXPOSITION GROUNDS WITH THE AUDITORIUM, PARTHENON AND COMMERCE BUILDINGS IN BACKGROUND.

Robert B. Field, Anthony Fiala and William B. Bryant. Three ex-members and two prospective members of the Twenty-third Regiment also accompanied the battalion.